I0409992

U.S. ENVIRONMENTAL PROTECTION AGENCY

OFFICE OF INSPECTOR GENERAL

Analysis of Office of Inspector General Policies and Procedures Addressing CIGIE Quality Standards

Report No. 12-N-0516   June 4, 2012

Scan this mobile code
to learn more about
the EPA OIG.

Report Contributors: Carolyn J. Hicks
Tina Lovingood
Kevin L. Christensen
Anthony Grear

Abbreviations

CIGIE	Council of the Inspectors General on Integrity and Efficiency
CPE	Continuing Professional Education
ECIE	Executive Council on Integrity and Efficiency
EPA	U.S. Environmental Protection Agency
IG	Inspector General
IO	Immediate Office
OA	Office of Audit
OC	Office of Counsel
OCOS	Office of the Chief of Staff
OCPA	Office of Congressional and Public Affairs
OI	Office of Investigations
OIG	Office of Inspector General
PCIE	President's Council on Integrity and Efficiency
PMH	Project Management Handbook
QA	Quality Assurance

Hotline

To report fraud, waste, or abuse, contact us through one of the following methods:

e-mail:	OIG_Hotline@epa.gov	write:	EPA Inspector General Hotline
phone:	1-888-546-8740		1200 Pennsylvania Avenue NW
fax:	202-566-2599		Mailcode 2431T
online:	http://www.epa.gov/oig/hotline.htm		Washington, DC 20460

At a Glance

Why We Did This Review

We analyzed U.S. Environmental Protection Agency (EPA) Office of Inspector General (OIG) policies and procedures addressing the Council of the Inspectors General on Integrity and Efficiency (CIGIE) *Quality Standards for Federal Offices of Inspector General* (Silver Book). We sought to determine whether the EPA OIG has adequate policies, procedures, and other guidance that will help ensure compliance with the CIGIE standards and to determine compliance with our own internal standards.

Background

CIGIE was statutorily established as an independent entity within the executive branch by the *Inspector General Reform Act of 2008*. The CIGIE mission is to address integrity, economy, and effectiveness issues that transcend individual government agencies; and to increase the professionalism and effectiveness of personnel by developing policies, standards, and approaches to aid in the establishment of a well-trained and highly skilled workforce in the offices of the Inspectors General.

For further information,
contact our **Office of Congressional and Public Affairs at (202) 566-2391.**

The full report is at:
www.epa.gov/oig/reports/2012/
20120604-12-N-0516.pdf

Analysis of Office of Inspector General Policies and Procedures Addressing CIGIE Quality Standards

What We Found

EPA OIG has policies and procedures or other guidance to satisfy Silver Book requirements in all except one area. The one area lacking guidance pertains to training for the auditors and evaluators and the responsibility of key managers to ensure their staff members have the skills necessary to match the OIG's needs.

We noted that 21 of the 28 policies and procedures reviewed, or 75 percent, are past the required review date prescribed by EPA OIG Policy 001, *OIG Directives System*. Of those 21 that are out of date, 48 percent are at least 3 years overdue for review/update.

We concluded that our Policy 503, *Allegations Against OIG Employees* (last approved September 2001), needs to be updated to be consistent with current law and provisions. Further, we concluded that additional policies and procedures need to be assessed by the responsible offices to determine whether they are subject to Silver Book requirements or are sufficient to meet those requirements. These policies and procedures cover management challenges; annual plans; training provided to the Agency on fraud, waste, abuse, and mismanagement; and the need for independent external peer reviews.

What We Recommend

We recommend that the Inspector General direct offices we identified as having policies, procedures, or other guidance past the required review date to update them. We also recommend that the Inspector General direct responsible offices to develop and issue necessary guidance and improve current guidance.

Inspector General's Response

The Inspector General agreed with all recommendations and directed the responsible OIG offices to provide specific milestone and/or completion dates for their respective policies highlighted in the report.

UNITED STATES ENVIRONMENTAL PROTECTION AGENCY
WASHINGTON, D.C. 20460

June 4, 2012

MEMORANDUM

SUBJECT: Analysis of Office of Inspector General Policies and Procedures
Addressing CIGIE Quality Standards
Report No. 12-N-0516

FROM: Anthony Grear, Auditor
Immediate Office (on detail)

TO: Arthur A. Elkins, Jr.
Inspector General

Attached is our final report on our analysis of Office of Inspector General (OIG) policies and procedures addressing the Council of the Inspectors General on Integrity and Efficiency (CIGIE) *Quality Standards for Federal Offices of Inspector General* (Silver Book). This analysis of whether our organization has adequate policies, procedures, and other guidance will help ensure our compliance with the CIGIE standards. For our review, we selected overarching CIGIE requirements and determined whether our policies and procedures met those requirements. We explain the details of our process in the "Scope and Methodology" section of this report.

In your response to the draft report, you agreed with all recommendations and directed that the responsible offices provide estimated completion dates to make the policies and procedures current. Those offices provided estimated completion dates, which can be found in the "Estimated Completion Dates for Recommendations" table in appendix A. We also made revisions to the report for factual and clarity purposes where appropriate.

If you have any questions about this report and its recommendations, please contact Carolyn Hicks at (202) 566-1238, Tina Lovingood at (202) 566-2906, Kevin Christensen at (202) 566-1007, or Anthony Grear at (202) 566-2541.

Table of Contents

Appendices

Purpose

The purpose of this review is to report the results of our analysis of whether U.S. Environmental Protection Agency (EPA) Office of Inspector General (OIG) policies, procedures, and other guidance conform with the Council of the Inspectors General on Integrity and Efficiency (CIGIE) *Quality Standards for Federal Offices of Inspector General* (Silver Book).[1] These standards are the overall quality framework for managing, operating, and conducting the work of OIGs and are intended to guide the Inspector General (IG) community's efforts. The objectives of this review were to determine whether EPA OIG:

- Has policies and procedures to help ensure compliance with the Silver Book.
- Policies and procedures in place are current based on the expected review date.

Background

The *Inspector General Reform Act of 2008* (P.L. 110-409), which amended the *Inspector General Act of 1978,* created the CIGIE by combining what were formerly known as the President's Council on Integrity and Efficiency (PCIE) and the Executive Council on Integrity and Efficiency (ECIE). The *Inspector General Reform Act of 2008* established CIGIE as an independent entity within the executive branch to:

- Address integrity, economy, and effectiveness issues that transcend individual government agencies; and
- Increase the professionalism and effectiveness of personnel by developing policies, standards, and approaches to aid in the establishment of a well-trained and highly skilled workforce in IG offices.

The Silver Book contains quality standards for the management, operation, and conduct of federal OIGs. The standards incorporate by reference the existing professional standards for audit, investigation, inspection, and evaluation efforts. OIGs have a special need for high standards of professionalism and integrity in light of the mission of the IGs under the Act. Because of this special need, the PCIE/ECIE adopted the general quality standards contained in the Silver Book.

The EPA OIG has developed Policy 001, *OIG Directives System,* to provide a framework for identifying, developing, reviewing, approving, and assessing internal OIG policies and procedures. EPA OIG policies and procedures are to be reviewed, at a minimum, every 3 years from the date of issuance and be either (1) reissued as is with a new approval date, (2) updated and reissued, or (3) rescinded. Offices shall revise their policies and procedures sooner if new regulations, requirements,

---

[1] http://www.ignet.gov/pande/standards/igstds.pdf

or processes dictate. IG Statements are in effect for 1 year from the date of issuance, at which time they must be reviewed by the IG or a designee and be either rescinded or incorporated into a new or existing EPA OIG policy or procedure.

In our quality assurance report *Measuring the Quality of Office of Inspector General Reports Issued in Fiscal Years 2008 and 2009* (Report No. 10-N-0134, issued June 2, 2010), we concluded that several recommendations from a February 2008 quality assurance report had been implemented and helped to improve the quality of reports and work processes. Although this current report is not designed to be a follow-up to that report, both discuss areas for improvement that are being addressed in a revision currently being undertaken of the EPA OIG's Policy 101, *Project Management Handbook* (PMH).

Noteworthy Achievements

During our analysis we identified areas where some offices have already taken steps to bring about necessary improvements. For example, the Office of Investigations expects to issue its hotline policy for internal review by the end of May 2012. The Office of Audit issued updated Policy and Procedure 102, regarding independence. With the revision to the *Government Auditing Standards* in December 2011, the Quality Assurance staff has begun a thorough review and updating process to make the 2008 PMH current. The Office of the Chief of Staff is developing a training policy and procedure that will address continuing professional education (CPE), among other topics.

Scope and Methodology

We performed this review from December 2011 to March 2012. The scope of work performed does not constitute an audit under generally accepted government auditing standards. This review compared EPA OIG policies and procedures with the October 2003 Silver Book. The review involved a study of the Silver Book and the identification of significant requirements in areas including ethics, internal controls, quality assurance, and human capital. Through our analysis we identified 14 overarching requirements related to our work and cross-referenced them to 28 policies, procedures, and other EPA OIG guidance (see appendix B). These policies and procedures were the responsibility of the following OIG offices:

- Office of Audit (OA)
- Office of Congressional and Public Affairs (OCPA)
- Office of Counsel (OC)
- Office of Investigations (OI)
- Office of the Chief of Staff (OCOS), in the Immediate Office (IO)
- Quality Assurance (QA), also in the IO

No Office of Program Evaluation or Office of Mission Systems policies and procedures, within the scope of our review, relate to the standards established by the Silver Book.

We evaluated OIG policies and procedures current as of December 31, 2011, to determine whether or to what extent they addressed the Silver Book requirements. We also took note of policies and procedures past the required review date (out of date). Because of the highly technical nature of investigation functions, we suggest that OI perform its own review of its significant policies and procedures that may be subject to Silver Book requirements for independent external reviews.

Results of Review

Policies and Procedures Out of Date

We noted that 21 of the 28 policies and procedures reviewed, or 75 percent, are past the required review date. Of those 21 that are out of date, 48 percent are at least 3 years overdue for review/update. Table 1 provides a breakdown by type of guidance; table 2 provides a breakdown by office.

Table 1: Out-of-date guidance (by type)

Status by type	Policies	Proc.	IG stmts.	Other internal	Totals	% of totals
OIG guidance reviewed	20	5	2	1*	28	
OIG guidance out of date	15	4	2	0	21	75%
Guidance at least 3 years out of date	6	3	1	0	10	48%

Source: OIG analysis.

*Personal Impairment Form

Table 2: Out-of-date guidance (by office)

Status by office	OCOS (IO)	OI	QA (IO)	OC	OA	OCPA	Totals
OIG guidance reviewed	9	9	4	4	1	1	28
OIG guidance out of date	9	8	3	1	0	0	21
Guidance at least 3 years out of date	3	5	1	1	0	0	10

Source: OIG analysis.

New Policy and Procedure Needed

We found that EPA OIG has policies and procedures or other guidance to satisfy the overarching Silver Book requirements we identified in all areas except one (a list of the requirements and our conclusions is in appendix B). The OIG lacks an office-wide policy pertaining to training and the responsibility of key managers to ensure their staff members have the skills necessary to match the OIG's needs. We noted that OI has a detailed internal training policy (EPA OIG Policy 202, *Special Agent Training,* last approved July 2007). However, EPA OIG does not have a training policy and procedure in place for staff required to maintain CPE hours. According to the Silver Book:

> To ensure that the OIG staff members collectively possess needed skills, the Inspector General and key managers should assess the skills of their staff members and determine the extent to which these skills match the OIG's requirements. OIG management is responsible for deciding the methods by which identified needs can be met by hiring contractors or outside consultants, using staff members who possess the requisite skills, developing staff members and providing training, or recruiting new staff. Each OIG must also ensure that staff members meet the requirements for continuing professional education contained in the applicable professional standards.

OCOS is developing a training policy and procedure that will likely address areas of this Silver Book requirement not covered by existing guidance. The new policy and procedure will need to ensure:

- Staff members possess needed skills
- Managers assess skills to match OIG requirements
- Management decides upon methods to meet OIG requirements
- Staff meets CPE requirements.

We met with OCOS on February 22, 2012, to discuss the roles of an EPA OIG training officer and items we believe the new training policy and procedure need to address. It is our understanding that only a policy document will be issued initially, with a procedures document to follow.

Policy Needs Updating

We identified one area where our current guidance should be updated to be consistent with a change in law. According to the Silver Book, Executive Order 12993, *Administrative Allegations Against Inspectors General,* provides an independent investigative mechanism to ensure that administrative allegations against IGs and OIG senior staff are expeditiously investigated and resolved. The *Inspector General Reform Act of 2008* (P.L. 110-409 of October 14, 2008,

122 Stat. 4302) (IG Reform Act) established that CIGIE is to have an Integrity Committee tasked with reviewing allegations of wrongdoing received against an IG or a OIG staff member. CIGIE adopted policies and procedures for the Integrity Committee in 2009. This statutorily-created Integrity Committee assumes the responsibilities of the Integrity Committee that functioned previously under Executive Orders 12805, *Integrity and Efficiency in Federal Programs*, and 12993. EPA OIG Policy 503, *Allegations Against OIG Employees* (last approved September 2001), addresses allegations against the IG and senior OIG staff. However, the policy needs to be updated to include appropriate references to the IG Reform Act and current Integrity Committee policies and procedures.

Policies and Procedures Need to Be Assessed by Responsible Offices

The following three additional areas need to be assessed by the responsible offices to determine whether they are sufficient to meet Silver Book requirements:

- **Management challenges (OA).** EPA OIG Policy 009, *OIG Strategic Plan Policy,* mentions management challenges, but neither the policy nor the corresponding procedure addresses specific steps to develop/prepare them (see appendix B, item #7).

- **Annual plan (OCOS).** While the OIG has EPA OIG Policy 009, *OIG Strategic Plan Policy,* and EPA OIG Policy 010, *Two Year Assignment Plan Policy,* the OIG does not have an annual plan policy as required by the Silver Book (see appendix B, item #8, requirement 3).

- **Training Agency on fraud, waste, abuse, and mismanagement (OI).** According to the Silver Book, "OIG planning should develop a strategy to identify the causes of fraud, waste, abuse, and mismanagement in high-risk agency programs, and to help agencies implement a system of management improvements to overcome these problems" (see appendix B, item #9). There is no EPA OIG policy to document the details of the OIG's strategy. However, we met with OI staff and were provided copies of instructive brochures and were informed that posters are placed throughout EPA facilities. We verified that these brochures are accessible at EPA's public Web site. We were also informed that OI performs some briefings for the Agency in these areas.

We also identified six significant investigations-related policies and procedures that appear to be subject to Silver Book requirements for independent external review. According to the Silver Book, "Independent external reviews are conducted by sources not assigned to the unit being reviewed. These reviews are distinct from ongoing management and supervision, and encompass the entirety of internal control, including administrative operations and professional services (audits, investigations, inspections, and evaluations)" (see appendix B, item #5).

Following are the six key OI policies and procedures already in place that we believe are subject to independent external review:

- EPA OIG Policy 201, *Authority and Responsibility of Special Agents* (last approved March 2007)
- EPA OIG Policy 204, *Firearms and Law Enforcement Equipment* (last approved December 2009)
- EPA OIG Policy and Procedure 206, *Case Administration* (last approved April 2005)
- EPA OIG Policy 208, *Confidential Funds, Sources of Information, and Confidential Informants* (last approved April 2008)
- EPA OIG Policy and Procedure 209, *Technical Surveillance* (last approved June 2005)
- EPA OIG Policy 210, *Undercover Operations* (last approved September 2008)

In our meeting with OI, we determined that OI undergoes external peer reviews every 3 years. Based on a July 2011 review of OI's operations, including the policies and procedures aforementioned, OI was found to be in compliance with the quality standards established by CIGIE and the Attorney General's guidelines. However, although the policies and procedures appear sufficient in substance, they still need to be updated according to EPA OIG Policy 001, *OIG Directives System.*

Recommendations

We recommend that the Inspector General:

1. Direct the offices of OA, OC, OCOS, OI, and QA to refer to appendix B to identify policies and procedures they are responsible for reviewing to ensure the policies and procedures are up to date according to EPA OIG Policy 001, *OIG Directives System.*

2. Direct OCOS to finalize and issue training policy and procedures that include, among other issue areas, instructions about CPEs (see appendix B, item #12, "Training Policy").

3. Direct OC to update EPA OIG Policy 503, *Allegations Against OIG Employees,* to include appropriate references to the *Inspector General Reform Act of 2008* and current procedures for handling allegations (see appendix B, item #1).

4. Direct offices to assess whether policies and/or procedures need to be developed for management challenges (OA); an annual plan (OCOS); and training of the Agency on fraud, waste, abuse, and mismanagement (OI).

IG Response and QA Evaluation

The IG agreed with all recommendations and directed OA, OC, OCOS, OI, and QA to provide specific milestone and/or completion dates for their respective policies highlighted in the report.

With regard to recommendation 3, OC is revising Policy 503 in its entirety to capture IG Reform Act requirements, and other organizational changes that have taken place within the OIG.

For recommendation 4, we were informed that OA will develop an EPA OIG policy and procedure on developing top management challenges. Regarding training of the Agency on fraud, waste, abuse, and mismanagement, we concluded after meeting with OI that there is sufficient evidence of providing instruction to the Agency and the general public on these areas.

In our draft report, we recommended that OI assess its significant policies and procedures to determine whether the activity is subject to Silver Book requirements for independent external reviews. We met with OI and confirmed that OI undergoes an external peer review every 3 years. Part of this assessment includes a review of its policies and procedures for compliance with CIGIE and IG Act guidelines. OI successfully completed the most recent assessment, which was reported in July 2011. Based on the results of this assessment, we concluded that the OI policies and procedures we noted in this report were covered by the peer review and therefore warranted a removal of a fifth recommendation that had been in the draft report.

Estimated Completion Dates
for Recommendations

Recommendation	Description	Action Office	Estimated Completion Date
1. Direct the offices of OA, OC, OCOS, OI, and QA to refer to appendix B to identify policies and procedures they are responsible for reviewing to ensure the policies and procedures are up to date according to EPA OIG Policy 001, OIG Directives System.	Policy 503, Allegations Against OIG Employees	OC	8/15/12
	Policy 009, OIG Strategic Plan Policy	OCOS	6/30/12
	Policy 010, Two Year Assignment Plan Policy (Annual Plan)	OCOS	6/30/12
	Policy 013, OIG Review of Regulations and Agency Directives	OCOS	9/30/12
	Policy 301, Student Loan Repayment Program	OCOS	Completed
	Policy 307, Workforce Diversity	OCOS	12/20/12
	Policy 317, Documenting Training in the Training Information System	OCOS	6/30/12
	Policy 319, Workforce Planning	OCOS	9/30/12
	Procedure 009, Strategic Planning Process	OCOS	6/30/12
	Procedure 319, Workforce Planning: Guidance and Procedures for the OIG	OCOS	9/30/12
	Policy 201, Authority and Responsibility of Special Agents	OI	9/30/12
	Policy 206, Case Administration	OI	9/30/12
	Policy 208, Confidential Funds and Sources of Information and Confidential Informants	OI	9/30/12
	Policy 209, Technical Surveillance	OI	9/30/12
	Policy 210 ,Undercover Operations	OI	9/30/12
	Policy 610, Hotline Policy	OI	9/30/12
	Procedure 206, Case Administration	OI	9/30/12
	Procedure 209, Technical Surveillance	OI	9/30/12
	IG Statement No. 2, Measuring the Quality of Audit, Evaluation and Public Liaison Assignments	QA	7/31/12
	IG Statement No. 5, Completing and Archiving Assignments in AutoAudit	QA	7/31/12
	Policy 101, Project Management Handbook	QA	7/31/12
2. Direct OCOS to finalize and issue training policy and procedures that include, among other issue areas, instructions about CPEs (see appendix B, Item 12, "Training Policy").	Training policy	OCOS	6/30/12
	Training procedure	OCOS	6/30/12
3. Direct OC to update EPA OIG Policy 503, Allegations Against OIG Employees, to include appropriate references to the *Inspector General Reform Act of 2008* and current procedures for handling allegations (see appendix B, item 1).	Policy 503, Allegations Against OIG Employees	OC	8/15/12
4. Direct offices to assess whether policies and/or procedures need to be developed for management challenges (OA); an annual plan (OCOS); and training of the Agency on fraud, waste, abuse, and mismanagement (OI).	Management Challenges	OA	9/30/12
	Annual Plan	OCOS	6/30/12
	Training Agency on fraud, waste, abuse, and mismanagement	OI	Completed

Analysis of OIG Policies and Procedures Addressing Overarching Silver Book Requirements

EXPLANATION:

	Policies and/or procedures that are yet to be developed or issued.
	Policies and/or procedures out of date by at least 3 years.
	Policies and/or procedures out of date by less than 3 years.
	External guidance.
Yes*	IG Statement #2 will be incorporated into the PMH currently under revision and when all working group recommendations are approved and implementation begins (Scorecard). IG Statement #5 will be terminated once the procedures are incorporated into the PMH currently under revision.

Item #	Requirement for OIG Policies (Quoted from Silver Book)	Citation in Silver Book	OIG Policy/Procedure Number	Respons. Office	REVIEW DATES			Comments/Resolution
					Last Updated	Update Due	Review Overdue?	
1	Executive Order 12993 ("Administrative Allegations Against Inspectors General") provides an independent investigative mechanism to ensure that administrative allegations against IGs and OIG senior staff are expeditiously investigated and resolved. The order establishes a PCIE/ECIE Integrity Committee to receive, review, and refer such allegations. OIGs should maintain policies and controls to ensure that allegations are handled consistent with the executive order. OIGs should also have in place policies and procedures to ensure that criminal allegations against the IG or senior OIG staff are appropriately referred to the Attorney General.	Section B., pdf page 11/48	Policy 503 Allegations Against OIG Employees http://oigintra/policy/documents/OIGPolicy503.pdf	OC	09/01/01	09/01/04	Yes	Policy needs to be updated to reflect and refer to *Inspector General Reform Act of 2008*, and 2009 Integrity Committee procedures, which supersedes Executive Order 12993.
2	Personal impairments of staff members result from relationships and beliefs that might cause OIG staff members to limit the extent of an inquiry, limit disclosure, or weaken or slant their work in any way. OIG staff are responsible for notifying the appropriate officials within their organization if they have any personal impairments to independence.	Section 2., pdf page 13/48	Policy 501 Standards of Conduct http://oigintra/policy/documents/Policy501StandardsofConduct.FINAL.signed9-30-11.pdf	OC	09/30/11	09/30/14	No	Appears sufficient.

Item #	Requirement for OIG Policies (Quoted from Silver Book)	Citation in Silver Book	OIG Policy/Procedure Number	Respons. Office	REVIEW DATES			Comments/Resolution
					Last Updated	Update Due	Review Overdue?	
			Procedure 501 Standards of Conduct http://oigintra/policy/documents/Procedure501StandardsofConduct.FINAL.signed 9-30-11.pdf	OC	09/30/11	09/30/14	No	Appears sufficient.
			Personal Impairments Forms http://oigintra/DocumentLibrary/documents/Impairments_Form.pdf	OC	n/a	n/a	n/a	Appears sufficient.
			Policy 102 OIG Independence http://oigintra/policy/documents/Policy102finalsigned20 07.pdf	OA	04/03/12	04/03/15	No	Appears sufficient.
3	Factors external to the OIG may restrict the work or interfere with an OIG's ability to form independent and objective opinions and conclusions. External impairments to independence occur when the OIG staff is deterred from acting objectively and exercising professional skepticism by pressures, actual or perceived, from management and employees of the reviewed entity or oversight organizations. OIGs should have policies and procedures in place to resolve or report external impairments to independence when they exist.	Section 3., pdf page 14/48	Policy 102 OIG Independence http://oigintra/policy/documents/Policy102finalsigned20 07.pdf	OA	04/03/12	04/03/15	No	2011 Government Auditing Standards (Yellow Book) Section 3.14e Appears sufficient

| Item # | Requirement for OIG Policies (Quoted from Silver Book) | Citation in Silver Book | OIG Policy/Procedure Number | Respons. Office | REVIEW DATES | | | Comments/Resolution |
					Last Updated	Update Due	Review Overdue?	
4	The Inspector General should provide for an assessment of the risks the OIG faces from both external and internal sources. Risk assessment includes identifying and analyzing relevant risks associated with achieving the OIG's objectives, such as those defined in strategic and annual performance plans, and forming a basis for determining how risks should be managed. Risk assessment methodologies and the formality of their documentation may vary from OIG to OIG, depending on the OIG's size, mission, and other factors.	Section D. pdf page 20/48	Procedure 009 Strategic Planning Process http://oigintra/policy/documents/OPAR-07.pdf	OCOS (IO)	06/25/04	06/25/06	Yes	Appears sufficient but could better explain risk management methodologies. Risk assessment covered in PMH.
			Policy 009 OIG Strategic Plan Policy http://oigintra/policy/documents/policy28.pdf	OCOS (IO)	06/16/03	06/16/06	Yes	Appears sufficient but could better explain risk management methodologies. Risk assessment covered in PMH.
			Policy 010 Two Year Assignment Plan Policy http://oigintra/policy/documents/OIG_21_000.pdf	OCOS (IO)	10/13/04	10/13/07	Yes	Appears sufficient but could better explain risk management methodologies. Risk assessment covered in PMH.
			Policy 101 Project Management Handbook http://oigintra/policy/documents/Policy101.PMH.Final.05.08.08.pdf (applies to OPE, OA, and OMS)	QA (IO)	05/08/08	05/08/11	Yes	Appears sufficient. PMH currently in revision process.

Item #	Requirement for OIG Policies (Quoted from Silver Book)	Citation in Silver Book	OIG Policy/Procedure Number	Respons. Office	REVIEW DATES			Comments/Resolution
					Last Updated	Update Due	Review Overdue?	
5	Independent external reviews are conducted by sources not assigned to the unit being reviewed. These reviews are distinct from ongoing management and supervision, and encompass the entirety of internal control, including administrative operations and professional services (audits, investigations, inspections, and evaluations). Quality assurance is intended to assess the internal controls of the entire OIG or specific OIG components. The Quality Assurance Program is a type of independent review that focuses on complying with professional standards in conducting professional services (see the Maintaining Quality Assurance standard).	Section 3., pdf page 22/48	Policy 101 Project Management Handbook http://oigintra/policy/documents/Policy101.PMH.Final.05.08.08.pdf (applies to OPE, OA, and OMS)	QA (IO)	05/08/08	05/08/11	Yes	Appears sufficient PMH currently in revision process.
			Policy 006 OIG Quality Assurance Program http://oigintra/policy/documents/Policy006QualityAssuranceProgram.Final.signed.07-21-11_000.pdf	QA (IO)	07/21/11	07/21/14	No	Current and up to date.
			IG Statement No. 2 Measuring the Quality of Audit, Evaluation and Public Liaison Assignments http://oigintra/policy/documents/IGStmtNo.210-10-06.pdf	QA (IO)	10/10/06	10/10/07	Yes*	Scorecard guidance. This policy will be updated after the PMH is finalized.
			IG Statement No. 5 Completing and Archiving Assignments in AutoAudit http://oigintra/policy/documents/IGStmtNo.505-12-10.pdf	QA (IO)	05/12/10	05/12/11	Yes*	IG Statements will terminate upon the updating of the PMH currently under revision.

Item #	Requirement for OIG Policies (Quoted from Silver Book)	Citation in Silver Book	OIG Policy/Procedure Number	Respons. Office	REVIEW DATES			Comments/Resolution
					Last Updated	Update Due	Review Overdue?	
			Standards that apply for investigation's external peer reviews (CIGIE) found at http://www.ignet.gov/pande/standards/invprg0509.doc	n/a	n/a	n/a	n/a	
			Policy 201 Authority and Responsibility of Special Agents http://oigintra/policy/documents/Policy2013-18-2007.pdf	OI	03/28/07	03/28/10	Yes	Covered under external peer review completed July 2011.
			Policy 204 Firearms and Law Enforcement Equipment http://oigintra/policy/documents/Policy204Firearms12-08-2009.pdf	OI	12/08/09	12/09/12	No	Covered under external peer review completed July 2011.
			Policy 206 Case Administration http://oigintra/policy/documents/OI-206POLICY.pdf	OI	04/26/05	04/26/07	Yes	Covered under external peer review completed July 2011.
			Procedure 206 Case Administration (including sections 1-8) http://oigintra/policy/documents/OI-06PROCEDURE.pdf	OI	04/26/05	04/26/07	Yes	Covered under external peer review completed July 2011

| Item # | Requirement for OIG Policies (Quoted from Silver Book) | Citation in Silver Book | OIG Policy/Procedure Number | Respons. Office | REVIEW DATES | | | Comments/Resolution |
					Last Updated	Update Due	Review Overdue?	
			Policy 208 Confidential Funds and Sources of Information and Confidential Informants http://oigintra/policy/documents/Policy208ConfidentialFunds.fianl.pdf	OI	04/24/08	04/24/11	Yes	Covered under external peer review completed July 2011.
			Policy 209 Technical Surveillance http://oigintra/policy/documents/policy209_002.pdf	OI	06/02/05	06/02/07	Yes	Covered under external peer review completed July 2011.
			Procedure 209 Technical Surveillance http://oigintra/policy/documents/procedure09_002.pdf	OI	06/02/05	06/02/07	Yes	Covered under external peer review completed July 2011.
			Policy 210 Undercover Operations http://oigintra/policy/documents/Policy210Undercover Operations.pdf	OI	09/18/08	09/18/11	Yes	Covered under external peer review completed July 2011.
			CIGIE's Guide for Conducting External Peer Reviews of the Audit Organizations of Federal Offices of Inspector General (Appendix A)	n/a	n/a	n/a	n/a	Results from Peer review evaluated.

Item #	Requirement for OIG Policies (Quoted from Silver Book)	Citation in Silver Book	OIG Policy/Procedure Number	Respons. Office	REVIEW DATES			Comments/Resolution
					Last Updated	Update Due	Review Overdue?	
6	Each OIG shall establish and maintain a quality assurance program to ensure that work performed adheres to established OIG policies and procedures; meets established standards of performance, including applicable professional standards; and is carried out economically, efficiently, and effectively.	Section A., pdf page 23/48	Policy 101 Project Management Handbook http://oigintra/policy/documents/Policy101.PMH.Final.05.08.08.pdf (applies to OPE, OA, and OMS)	QA (IO)	05/08/08	05/08/11	Yes	Appears sufficient. PMH currently in revision process.
			Policy 006 OIG Quality Assurance Program http://oigintra/policy/documents/Policy006QualityAssuranceProgram.Final.signed. 07-21-11_000.pdf	QA (IO)	07/21/11	07/21/14	No	Current and up to date.
			IG Statement No. 2 Measuring the Quality of Audit, Evaluation and Public Liaison Assignments http://oigintra/policy/documents/IGStmtNo.210-10-06.pdf	QA (IO)	10/10/06	10/10/07	Yes*	Scorecard guidance. This policy will be updated after the PMH is finalized.
			IG Statement No. 5 Completing and Archiving Assignments in AutoAudit http://oigintra/policy/documents/IGStmtNo.505-12-10.pdf	QA (IO)	05/12/10	05/12/11	Yes*	IG Statements will terminate upon the updating of the PMH currently under revision.

12-N-0516

Item #	Requirement for OIG Policies (Quoted from Silver Book)	Citation in Silver Book	OIG Policy/Procedure Number	Respons. Office	REVIEW DATES			Comments/Resolution
					Last Updated	Update Due	Review Overdue?	
7	Each OIG shall maintain a planning system assessing the nature, scope, and inherent risks of agency programs and operations. This assessment forms the basis for establishing strategic and performance plans, including goals, objectives, and performance measures to be accomplished by the OIG within a specific time period.	Section A., pdf page 27/48	Procedure 009 Strategic Planning Process http://oigintra/policy/documents/OPAR-07.pdf	OCOS (IO)	06/25/04	06/25/06	Yes	Appears sufficient. Audit plans that consider risk are presented to Agency annually as well as management challenge assessments.
			Policy 009 OIG Strategic Plan Policy http://oigintra/policy/documents/policy28.pdf	OCOS (IO)	06/16/03	06/16/06	Yes	Appears sufficient
			Policy 010 Two Year Assignment Plan Policy http://oigintra/policy/documents/OIG_21_000.pdf	OCOS (IO)	12/13/04	12/13/07	Yes	Appears sufficient.
			Policy 101 Project Management Handbook http://oigintra/policy/documents/Policy101.PMH.Final.05.08.08.pdf (applies to OPE, OA, and OMS)	QA (IO)	05/08/08	05/08/11	Yes	Appears sufficient. PMH currently in revision process.

16

12-N-0516

Item #	Requirement for OIG Policies (Quoted from Silver Book)	Citation in Silver Book	OIG Policy/Procedure Number	Respons. Office	REVIEW DATES			Comments/Resolution
					Last Updated	Update Due	Review Overdue?	
8	OIGs should develop an appropriate planning process, giving consideration to the following elements.

1. Use a strategic planning process that carefully considers current and emerging agency programs, operations, risks, and management challenges. This analysis will identify the nature of agency programs and operations, their performance measures and anticipated outcomes, their scope and dollar magnitude, their staffing and budgetary trends, their perceived vulnerabilities, and their inherent risks.

2. Develop a methodology and process for identifying and prioritizing agency programs and operations as potential subjects for audit, investigation, inspection, or evaluation. The methodology should be designed to use the most effective combination of OIG resources, including previous OIG work and input from OIG staff. Also, the OIG should consider the plans of other organizations both internal and external to the agency.

3. Use an annual performance planning process that identifies the activities to audit, investigate, inspect, or evaluate and translates these priorities into outcome-related goals, objectives, and performance measures. As part of this planning process, OIGs should consider agency actions to address recommendations from prior OIG work. Because resources are rarely sufficient to meet requirements, the OIG must choose among competing needs. | Section B., pdf page 28/48 | Procedure 009 Strategic Planning Process

http://oigintra/policy/documents/OPAR-07.pdf | OCOS (IO) | 06/25/04 | 06/25/06 | Yes | Appears sufficient. |
| | | | Policy 009 OIG Strategic Plan Policy

http://oigintra/policy/documents/policy28.pdf | OCOS (IO) | 06/16/03 | 06/16/06 | Yes | Appears sufficient. |

12-N-0516

Item #	Requirement for OIG Policies (Quoted from Silver Book)	Citation in Silver Book	OIG Policy/Procedure Number	Respons. Office	REVIEW DATES			Comments/Resolution
					Last Updated	Update Due	Review Overdue?	
			Policy 010 Two Year Assignment Plan Policy http://oigintra/policy/documents/OIG_21_000.pdf	OCOS (IO)	12/13/04	12/13/07	Yes	Appears sufficient. It is not clear at this point whether developing "outcome"-related goals is still the federal government plan since the Program Assessment Rating Tool (PART) process has been placed on hold.
			Policy 101 Project Management Handbook http://oigintra/policy/documents/Policy101.PMH.Final.05.08.08.pdf (applies to OPE, OA, and OMS)	QA (IO)	05/08/08	05/08/11	Yes	Appears sufficient. PMH currently in revision process.

Item #	Requirement for OIG Policies (Quoted from Silver Book)	Citation in Silver Book	OIG Policy/Procedure Number	Respons. Office	REVIEW DATES			Comments/Resolution
					Last Updated	Update Due	Review Overdue?	
9	OIG planning should develop a strategy to identify the causes of fraud, waste, abuse, and mismanagement in high-risk agency programs, and to help agencies implement a system of management improvements to overcome these problems. OIG prevention efforts may include the following:

1. A routine procedure for OIG staff to identify and report prevention opportunities as these may come up in their work, and for OIG managers to refer these to agency management, as appropriate;

2. Special awareness and training initiatives designed to alert agency employees to systemic weaknesses in the programs and operations of their agencies;

3. Review and comment on initial design of new agency programs and operations;

4. Analyses of audit, investigative, and other OIG reports to identify trends and patterns;

5. Education and training to ensure that appropriate OIG staff have requisite abilities in the loss prevention area, as well as fraud detection and prevention; and

6. An effective means for tracking the implementation of recommendations. | Section D., pdf page 30-31/48 | Policy 101 Project Management Handbook

http://oigintra/policy/docum ents/Policy101.PMH.Final.0 5.08.08.pdf | QA (IO) | 05/08/08 | 05/08/11 | Yes | Appears sufficient.

PMH currently in revision process. |
| 10 | The Inspector General should timely advise department and agency heads, consistent with requirements of confidentiality, of any agency official who attempts to impede or fails to require a contractor under his or her responsibility to desist from impeding an audit, investigation, inspection, evaluation, or any other OIG activity. | Section B.2., pdf page 32/48 | Policy 102 OIG Independence

http://oigintra/policy/docum ents/Policy102finalsigned20 07.pdf | OA | 04/03/12 | 04/03/15 | No | |

Item #	Requirement for OIG Policies (Quoted from Silver Book)	Citation in Silver Book	OIG Policy/Procedure Number	Respons. Office	REVIEW DATES			Comments/Resolution
					Last Updated	Update Due	Review Overdue?	
11	Each OIG's process for ensuring that its staff members possess the requisite qualifications should encompass processes for recruiting, hiring, continuously developing, training, and evaluating their staff members, and succession planning to assist the organization in maintaining a workforce that has the ability to meet the OIG's mission.	Section B., pdf page 36/48	Policy 319 Workforce Planning http://oigintra/policy/documents/Policy319WorkforcePlanningPolicy.pdf	OCOS (IO)	03/20/06	03/20/09	Yes	Policy needs new office titles, etc.
			Procedure 319 Workforce Planning: Guidance and Procedures for the OIG http://oigintra/policy/documents/Procedure319WorkforcePlanningGuidance.pdf	OCOS (IO)	03/20/06	03/20/09	Yes	Requires additional analysis by responsible office.
			Policy 307 Workforce Diversity http://oigintra/policy/documents/Policy307Diversity.pdf	OCOS (IO)	03/28/06	03/28/09	Yes	
			Policy 301 Student Loan Repayment Program http://oigintra/policy/documents/Policy301StudentLoanRepayment.final.pdf	OCOS (IO)	01/14/08	01/14/11	Yes	

Item #	Requirement for OIG Policies (Quoted from Silver Book)	Citation in Silver Book	OIG Policy/Procedure Number	Respons. Office	REVIEW DATES			Comments/Resolution
					Last Updated	Update Due	Review Overdue?	
12	To ensure that the OIG staff members collectively possess needed skills, the Inspector General and key managers should assess the skills of their staff members and determine the extent to which these skills match the OIG's requirements. OIG management is responsible for deciding the methods by which identified needs can be met by hiring contractors or outside consultants, using staff members who possess the requisite skills, developing staff members and providing training, or recruiting new staff. Each OIG must also ensure that staff members meet the requirements for continuing professional education contained in the applicable professional standards.	Section D., pdf page 37/48	Policy 319 Workforce Planning http://oigintra/policy/documents/Policy319WorkforcePlanningPolicy.pdf	OCOS (IO)	03/20/06	03/20/09	Yes	Policy needs new office titles, etc.
			Procedure 319 Workforce Planning: Guidance and Procedures for the OIG http://oigintra/policy/documents/Procedure319WorkforcePlanningGuidance.pdf	OCOS (IO)	03/20/06	03/20/09	Yes	No mention of CPEs in the policies and procedures listed.
			Policy 307 Workforce Diversity http://oigintra/policy/documents/Policy307Diversity.pdf	OCOS (IO)	03/28/06	03/28/09	Yes	Appears sufficient.
			Policy 301 Student Loan Repayment Program http://oigintra/policy/documents/Policy301StudentLoanRepayment.final.pdf	OCOS (IO)	01/14/08	01/14/11	Yes	Appears sufficient.

Item #	Requirement for OIG Policies (Quoted from Silver Book)	Citation in Silver Book	OIG Policy/Procedure Number	Respons. Office	REVIEW DATES			Comments/Resolution
					Last Updated	Update Due	Review Overdue?	
			Policy 317 Documenting Training in the Training Information System http://oigintra/policy/documents/Policy317TIS.pdf	OCOS (IO)	04/25/06	04/25/09	Yes	Will be rescinded when new training policy is issued.
			Training Policy (UNDER DEVELOPMENT)	OCOS (IO)	n/a	n/a	n/a	Policy is currently in development process. New policy will need to address skills, OIG requirements, and CPEs.
13	Each OIG shall establish and maintain a system to review and comment on existing and proposed legislation, regulations, and those directives that affect either the programs and operations of the OIG's agency or the mission and functions of the OIG. The system should result in OIG recommendations designed to (1) promote economy and efficiency in administering agency programs and operations; (2) prevent and detect fraud and abuse in such programs and operations; and (3) protect the integrity and independence of the OIG.	Section A., pdf page 38/48	Policy 611 OIG Legislative Review Policy http://oigintra/policy/documents/Policy611LegReview.signed10-26-09.pdf	OCPA	10/26/09	10/26/12	No	
			Policy 013 OIG Review of Regulations and Agency Directives http://oigintra/policy/documents/Policy013RegandDirectivesReview.05.06.08.pdf	OCOS (IO)	05/06/08	05/06/11	Yes	

Item #	Requirement for OIG Policies (Quoted from Silver Book)	Citation in Silver Book	OIG Policy/Procedure Number	Respons. Office	REVIEW DATES			Comments/Resolution
					Last Updated	Update Due	Review Overdue?	
14	Each OIG shall establish and follow policies and procedures for receiving and reviewing allegations. This system should ensure that an appropriate disposition, including appropriate notification, is made for each allegation.	Section A., pdf page 40/48	Policy 610 Hotline Policy http://oigintra/policy/docum ents/Policy610OIGHotlineP olicy12-28-2005.pdf	OI	12/28/05	12/28/07	Yes	Policy does not discuss appropriate disposition and how OI and other parts of the OIG will work together during an investigation and/or after a referral. According to OI staff, a draft is being processed.

23

12-N-0516

www.ingramcontent.com/pod-product-compliance
Lightning Source LLC
Chambersburg PA
CBHW081809280526
45789CB00008B/3070